OTHER BOOKS BY *Walter and Ingrid Trobisch*

Better Is Your Love Than Wine
I Loved a Girl
I Married You
The Joy of Being a Woman
Love Is a Feeling to Be Learned
Love Yourself
On Our Way Rejoicing

BOOKLETS BY *Walter Trobisch*
Martin Luther's Quiet Time
Spiritual Dryness

MY
BEAUTIFUL
FEELING

Correspondence
with Ilona

WALTER & INGRID
TROBISCH

InterVarsity Press
Downers Grove
Illinois 60515

InterVarsity Press is the book
publishing division of Inter-Varsity
Christian Fellowship, a student
movement active on campus at hundreds
of universities, colleges and
schools of nursing. For more
information about local and regional
activities, write IVCF, 233 Langdon St.,
Madison, WI 53703.

Library of Congress Catalog
Card Number: 76-21459
ISBN 0-87784-577-8

Printed in the United States
of America

The authors gratefully acknowledge
the help of Elisabeth Goldhor
and Marie de Putron in the translation
of this book from the original
German, Mein Schönes Gefühl.

Cover photo: Daniel Miller

CONTENTS

Prelude—a dialogue with the reader

You may well ask what motivated us to publish this rather personal correspondence. The reason is this. In our other books we simply mentioned in passing the problem of masturbation. To our great surprise we receive the majority of letters from our readers in response to these casual remarks.

Often these letters are desperate cries for help. This astonishes us since one hears and reads everywhere today that it is neither dangerous nor harmful to masturbate. Evidently this information is no help for those who have gotten started on this road. They long for a personal word.

They want to be taken seriously as individuals.

To satisfy their questions, we would have to engage in a lengthy correspondence with each one of them as we have with "Ilona." We would have to consider the circumstances in which each one lives, get acquainted with the people around them, discuss their experiences in the past and in the present and—last, but not least—consider the relationship of each one with God, learn the biography of their faith. This is not possible, unfortunately, since there are too many letters which share the problem of this mute pleasure.

This is why we have decided to publish a correspondence. Consider this book, therefore, as nothing more than the first letter written in response. Just imagine that you have written to us—or you would like to write to us—and now this book comes along. We agree, it is incomplete and it may leave some very personal questions unanswered—as is the case with every first answer. Yet it is longer, deeper and more detailed than a letter could be which was addressed to you alone.

We have to run the risk that one or the other of our readers will be introduced to problems which he has never met with himself. But we believe that this risk is smaller than the risk that those who need help are left in despair.

Desperation is expressed in many letters which reach us. This desperation is not simply the result of a repressive education which has produced guilt feelings. That explanation is too simple. Our impression is rather that the more the sexual taboos are breaking down, the more masturbation becomes a problem for individuals. The rational conclusion that objectively no harm is done evidently does not quench the subjective feeling of a shameful personal defeat. In spite of all the soothing arguments in favor of masturbation, few are really happy with it.

An impersonal essay, however, is of little value for those concerned. They are unable to identify themselves with it and do not feel personally addressed. Nor do they feel that they are being taken seriously in their special situation when they read an impersonal scientific treatise.

Therefore we entrust to you a correspondence. It is a real exchange of letters, not a fictional one. Ilona is a German girl and her letters have not been changed. At the beginning of the correspondence she was a high school senior, at the end a college freshman, majoring in English. That's why she was able to translate her own letters into English from the original German.

Our letters too remained basically as they were—even the dates and period of time between letters are authentic. In a few places we did some editing and added here and there a thought or an explanation. The books we refer to you will find in the notes. We recommend them if you want to gain more insight into the problem.

Ilona's personal data has been changed, of course, to make identification impossible.

This book deals in the first instance with one person only—the girl whom we call "Ilona." She lives in our midst. This is the way she has struggled through her problem. This is the way she has experienced help.

We hope that you will identify with Ilona's ups and downs, with her victories and defeats. We did not spare you the frustration of participating in these ups and downs, when territory that we thought had been won had to be given up again and a new start had to be made. This is the price we have to pay for publishing a true correspondence. If we had invented one, we could have offered you a more readable book with a steadily rising line. On the other hand, identification would have become very difficult for many who struggle with this problem.

You will also realize that some letters contradict each other. The reason is that Ilona went through a process of growth; in different stages of her development, different things were true and valid for her, different kinds of behavior adequate.

Therefore, it is irrelevant to quote statements from this book out of context in order to label it either "conservative" or "liberal." We know in advance that our comments will be too conservative for the "liberals" and too liberal for the "conservatives." But we believe we will be understood by those who leave behind their prejudices and take the trouble to empathize with Ilona and struggle along with her, letter by letter, just as we did.

Why did we choose Ilona?

First of all because she is a girl. The greatest number of letters sharing this problem reach us from females. It may also be more merciful to address young men (whose ego in general is more delicate and vulnerable than that of young women) in an indirect way by letting them read a girl's personal correspondence, in which their male problems are also pointed out especially when Ilona's boy friends appear on the scene.

Another reason we chose Ilona is her extraordinary ability to express herself. Her frankness and honesty, even when she fails, is so refreshing that we hope you will be able to love her as we do.

But the main reason for our choice was that Ilona is not a "special case" at all. Neither does she live in unusually difficult circumstances, nor is she neurotic in any sense. On the contrary, she is psychologically and physically a healthy, normal girl.

She has chosen her road herself. We have only accompanied her a certain distance. It is certainly not the road for everyone. Each human being is unique. God does not build serial houses—not even serial houses of counseling relationships.

Walter and Ingrid Trobisch
Lichtenberg 6
A—4880 St. Georgen I.A.
Austria

CORRESPONDENCE
WITH ILONA

**To the editor
"...." Magazine**

My name is Ilona. I am seventeen and a senior in high school. My great problem is that I do not live in peace with my sexuality. Again and again I satisfy my sexual desires myself, although I really don't want to do it. I can't seem to free myself from this drive and am unable to control it. Do you have any practical suggestions about how to learn this?

I am a Christian and know that God has given me my sexuality. Often I have prayed that I might be able to use this gift in the right way—in other words, to be patient and to concentrate on other things. But the desire seems always to be stronger than I. Since I give in again and again, I am worried for fear that I might do damage to myself, and maybe even to my future marriage. Half a year ago I didn't even know that girls could masturbate. I read about it in a sex manual and then, out of curiosity, I tried it.

The trouble is that I use masturbation as a compensation when I am frustrated because of a hard assignment for school or when I feel "down" for any other reason. Of course, masturbation does not help me either, but makes me feel still more frustrated and dissatisfied than ever. I keep telling myself how useless and stupid it is, but I keep doing it nevertheless. Am I sick? Am I abnormal?

I realize that sometimes I have difficulty disciplining myself in other areas too, for instance in my eating habits. Overeating can also be a way of escape for me when I don't feel like doing my homework.

Could you tell me how I can learn to master my needs and control my desires?

Many thanks that I could write to your magazine.

Ilona

October 18

Dear Ilona,

Your letter of October 2 was forwarded to my wife and me, and we were asked to reply. First of all we must say that you certainly have courage to write such a letter to a magazine. It's just your courage which gives us hope that we can have a good talk together. It may become a long talk, because there are no prefabricated answers applicable to any and every one in regard to your questions.

Before we can say very much, we have to get better acquainted with you and try to feel your life as you feel it. Therefore it would be good if you could tell us a little more about yourself, your family life—parents and brothers and sisters, if you have any. Do you belong to a youth group? Do you have a close girl friend? A boy friend? All these relationships we would have to think over together. The more concretely you can describe your situation, the better we can help you. We know very well that we are asking you to have a great deal of confidence in us, who are perfect strangers to you. It may help you to know that we have been married for twenty years and are parents of five children.

Just this much for today: You are not sick. Your letter gives us the impression that you are a normal, healthy girl.

What impresses us about you is your wide-awakeness and honesty.

Masturbation is not a sickness. It is a symptom, a sign of a deeper problem. You hint in this direction in your letter, and we congratulate you on how well you have observed yourself. The underlying problem is very often not sexual. It is just that the symptom has taken a sexual form.

Usually deep down, there is a feeling of dissatisfaction with oneself and with one's life, which one tries to overcome in a short moment of pleasure. But one does not succeed. The desired satisfaction is not reached. This you have experienced yourself.

It is precisely because the desired satisfaction is not reached that a person is tempted to repeat it. In this way a vicious circle is created. The more you are dissatisfied, the greater is the temptation; the more you give in, the more you are dissatisfied. The fetters grow tighter and tighter the more you try to shake them loose. In the end you are revolving only around yourself.

To recognize this may already help you to see the direction from which help can be expected. The more you get away from your own self, the more you think of others and occupy yourself with other interests, the less you will turn around yourself, and the temptation will be reduced.

We don't think you have to worry about your future marriage. Sometimes there may be a connection between masturbation and sexual inadequacy, but only when it has become a long and very frequent habit before marriage. Maybe we can go into this later on.

This is not your case now. After only half a year, when

it has supposedly happened infrequently, it has not yet become a habit. Still it is certainly not too soon to start to do something about it and to work together lest it become a habit for you.

Prayer is always helpful, if it is an expression of our fellowship with God. But there is also a kind of prayer which focuses on one point, on one single unfulfilled human desire. This is only a caricature of prayer. If you pray this way about masturbation, it does not help. It is like driving at night. When you look straight into the headlights of the oncoming car for fear of crashing into it, it is very likely that you may do just that.

Dear Mr. and Mrs. T.,

First of all I want to thank you very much for your letter. Every time during the last few days that I remembered it, I was filled with joy and thought, "Now you are no longer alone with your problem."

I had expected to receive some anonymous response as usually happens when you write to a magazine. Instead I received a letter from a married couple—and that was a special surprise for me.

I had feared one thing—that the answer would repeat what one can read everywhere nowadays: "Keep on doing it and stop worrying. It won't do you any harm. It might even be beneficial to your sexual development." All I know is that such advice does not help me because it contradicts a voice within me. So my conflict would only have deepened, had you answered me in this way.

The fact that you did not okay it was the first help in your letter. The second was that you did not offer a cut and dried answer, but rather you offered to "work together" with me. I accept your offer and am ready to do so.

The "advance in confidence" is not hard for me because I already know you from some of your books. Especially while reading *I Loved a Girl*, I thought to myself, "It would be good if I too could talk so openly with someone about sexual questions!" Now I can even do it with you!

My relationship to my parents is difficult to describe. My father is a businessman and is seldom home. Even when he is there, we rarely talk together, just the two of us. I am sure he means well and tries to take good care of his family. When I was small, I often sat on his lap. But during the last few years he has stopped touching me at all. Sometimes I think that he is afraid of that. Don't misunderstand me: We don't quarrel with each other. I certainly can't say that we have a bad relationship. I'd rather say that I don't have any relationship with him. I feel distant from him.

As my father was often away from home, my mother took over our training almost completely. I have two brothers and one sister. Mother was rather strict with us, and we did not have as much freedom as most of our classmates. That made us feel different from others. We never played games at home. Instead my mother took an active interest in our homework and put pressure on us to study hard for school. In a way we always felt forced. When she thought that we had not studied hard enough for a test on which we received a bad mark, we got a severe scolding. On the other hand, when we achieved high grades, it was only to be expected and we were rarely praised.

This one-sided focus on school achievement caused a lot of quarrels between my mother and me. When I wanted to be together with other young people, I had to do it more or less behind her back. When I went to our young people's fellowship or to choir practice (I enjoy singing), the question was always put to me, "Can you really afford to spend your time this way, right before your important exam?"

Lately the situation has improved somewhat, and I have more time for myself and freedom to do what I want. Recently I was even allowed to attend a weekend retreat which was fun for me.

I have lots of girl friends, one of whom is especially close to me. I also get along well with my sister and share confidences with her which I wouldn't feel free to tell my parents.

A boy friend? Well, I don't know whether I should answer yes or no. I think better no, because we've just broken up. We met at the home of another family. I was reluctant, because my first boy friend, who had taken the same dance course with me, had abandoned me, and since that time I had been afraid of another disappointment. But finally I accepted Martin's invitation for a walk. The third or fourth walk ended with embracing and kissing on a bench in the park. That was my first experience of this kind. I didn't even try to stop him because I had been longing for something like this for a long time.

Actually we had a wonderful time together and met rather often (my mother thought *too* often). We could talk to each other about everything, and of course there were always kisses and embraces too. In retrospect I realize that this physical attraction played a rather important role in our relationship. But we never went any further than that.

After the summer holidays other things became more important and I realized that my feelings for him were no longer so strong. When he sensed this and asked me about it, I felt that I must tell him the truth. I wasn't really sad about it except for his sake because he seemed quite hurt. I'm afraid that his feelings for me were stronger than my feelings for him from the very beginning. But I can't do anything about it. Or is there a way to help him?

This brings up a problem which has bothered me for some time. It's hard for me to feel at ease with boys. I attend an exclusive girls' school and so spend most of my time with girls. I am even affectionate with my best girl friend. Is that wrong?

My preoccupation with sex began only this year, actually even before I met Martin. I had decided to study the book, *Man and Woman* by Horst Wrage, and I found a reference there to female masturbation.[2] I learned that masturbation is regularly practiced by both sexes today. Supposedly it is simply a stage in healthy sexual development which is outgrown in time. Only if it is practiced too frequently would it be considered abnormal. This book said that it could cause neither physical nor psychological harm.

The feeling that results from a boy fondling his penis or a girl her clitoris was described as "a strange and pleasant stimulation, from mild to prickly."[3] Out of pure curiosity, I tried it. The beautiful feeling I experienced made me want to have it more often—and so it happened that I did it repeatedly.

However, there was also a "BUT" in the book: "But," it said, "young people should be aware of the fact that masturbation and the motives behind it could also be detrimental to normal development. This is always the case when it comes to an inner dependency upon masturbation so that one is unable to control it, in the same way that others are unable to control their desire for intercourse."[4]

"So it can be harmful after all?" I asked myself. Indeed on page 164, a possible negative effect was described: One could become conditioned to this special form of sexual stimulation; if practiced over a long period of time, it could lead to difficulties when having sexual intercourse later. That is why I asked you about the effects on marriage. Actually the book made these comments in reference to petting, but the form of stimulation is the same since petting is nothing more than mutual masturbation.

Well, the problem seemed to be solved when the friendship with Martin began. During this time, I never had the desire to do it. But then after the summer vacation it began again. I am afraid that it happens more frequently than you might think according to my first letter. I realize now that I have fallen into the exact trap against which the book warned. Gradually I have grown more and more dependent upon masturbation. I am afraid that it is already hindering my development, and that's why I wrote to the magazine.

It is always the same: After I have masturbated, I have no more desire whatsoever for a few days. But then the desire creeps in and dominates my thoughts until I am compelled once again to do it.

You mentioned the example of driving a car at night. I am aware that it starts with an idea which soon becomes a preoccupation: "Why not do it once again?" Yes, in this way I do stare into the headlights of the oncoming car. But I am unable to turn my eyes elsewhere. It is as if I am compelled to stare in this direction. My whole mind and body is captivated by this one thought and desire. So I get stuck in a rut.

How can I free myself from it? What is it that I really want to satisfy? Is it my sexual desire? Or is it something else?

I have tried everything under the sun, like trying to concentrate more on my studies. But after a few hours the compulsion is there again—and in order to get rid of it I give in. I observed that I am especially tempted after a test when I am completely exhausted and glad to be finished or—as I told you already—when I get stuck on a homework problem and become frustrated.

On the surface masturbation is something beautiful for me which I want to experience. But deep down it is a burden. Every time that I give in I feel guilty, even though no one ever forbade me to do it. It seems to me that Wrage's book should have taken care of any possible guilt feelings, but nevertheless they are there. Where do they come from?

You asked me to tell you what my absorbing interests or hobbies are. But I can't seem to think of any. Everything interests me to a certain degree, but nothing especially. This is also reflected in my school achievement record. Perhaps herein lies the root of my problem?

I guess my letter is long enough now. I hope you can understand what I am trying to say. Thank you for listening.

November 4

Dear Ilona,

We agree with you: The fact that you are not completely taken up or absorbed by any field of interest certainly might have something to do with your problem. Because of this a vacuum is created which you try to fill.

Yes, it is your sexual desire which you try to satisfy, but you do it in a very immature way. This is why you never succeed in being really satisfied. You see, sexuality is language. It is supposed to be a means of communication, addressed to another person. It wants to talk.

But instead you direct it toward yourself. In this way you hinder the process of becoming mature. The desire calls out into an empty room and only silence answers. So it calls out again and again until it becomes an expression of your being alone with yourself—not words directed to another, but mere lust directed toward oneself. It is this lack of communication[5] which you sense when asking, "Is not sexual desire something more than this?"

Your heart remains unsatisfied. It longs for a relationship. A relationship, however, is never established through masturbation. On the other hand, as long as you had a relationship with Martin, the temptation was gone. Also when you helped conduct that camp and discovered new abilities, your desire was stilled—but on a different level.

By the way, the only time when you mentioned in your letter that you had fun was at this camp. Having fun is probably the best weapon (tool) against your so-called being "stuck in a rut." You should allow yourself to have fun much more often.

Since your mother was so strict, you probably did not have enough fun in your childhood. Undoubtedly she meant well, and yet she appeared to you as someone who forced her will upon you without warmth and without giving you the feeling of being loved—which is the heart's desire of every child.

Could it be that for you masturbation became a way of solving this conflict? It gave you a chance to achieve some kind of satisfaction without needing your mother. Unconsciously perhaps in this way you wanted to prove to yourself your independence and freedom. What do you think? Are we feeling our way here in the right direction?

In any case it is a fact that for girls masturbation has something to do with the mother-relationship. The more a girl senses her mother as unfriendly, cool, distant, maybe even egocentric, the more frequent will be her temptation to masturbate.[6]

The relationship to the father is also important for the sexual development of the daughter, but it will affect more her sexual experience in marriage. Above all else a father must give his daughter the feeling that she can rely on him. By the way, he does not create this feeling by letting her do whatever she feels like doing, but rather by being strict and by giving her clear directions. Even if she rebels, the feeling remains: My father cares for me; I can rely upon him. Later on then in marriage, it will not be difficult to trust her husband, to believe that he is reliable, which is important for her sexual fulfillment.[7]

But you see, the relationship to your father is not destroyed. It has simply not yet been developed. And the relationship to your mother could certainly be improved. We feel that all these possibilities are still open in your situation. They are like marble blocks in the workshop of a sculptor, just waiting to be chiseled.

When others write to us about masturbation, they are often the only child in a family or have lost either their father or mother, or maybe both. Often they are persons without a real home, with few friends, and they may also lack the ability to make contact easily with others. Here it is much more difficult to help, although there are often unused possibilities.

You seem to us, however, to be rather an outgoing person who finds it easy to make contact with others. You have parents who love you, brothers and sisters, girl friends—and even a very close one. In addition to this you have a group of friends with whom you can have fun!

So we would say, by all means be with your friends as often as you can, go to your youth group, sing in your choir out of a full heart and do the things you really like to do. Can you play an instrument? Do you have a favorite game? How about a visit to a good play or movie? What about sports? Ballroom dancing?

And if your mother asks you whether you have time or money to do these things, then you say, "Not only can I afford to do them, I have to do them if I want to achieve my best in school." Prove to your mother that you are independent in this positive way, by this fruitful contradiction instead of masturbating.

Don't you think you could have a good talk with your mother and say, "Mom, why couldn't I sometimes be in charge of the cooking and baking? Or take over the household for a weekend?" That would be a creative way to achieve this wonderful feeling of independence.

And your father! After all you have one and he loves you! Can't you take the initiative and give him a hug and kiss when he comes home from a business trip? Would you consider it out of the way to tell him, "I like it when you stroke my hair?" or "Why don't you come and tell me good night as you did when I was small?" Maybe he needs some encouragement and waits secretly for a hint.

And then there are your brothers. They can probably help you the most to overcome your self-consciousness in the presence of guys. This self-consciousness is, by the way, very natural and normal—just as it is natural and normal to be affectionate with your girl friend. In order that you can understand these feelings better, we would like to explain this a little bit more.

All of us go through three phases in our development —one when we are in love with ourselves, another when we feel more drawn to the same sex and a third when we become capable of the difficult encounter with the other sex.

We go through the first phase before the age of five and we enter it again at the beginning of puberty.[8] The experience of "falling in love" or of "having a crush" is typical for this phase. We actually project our own image onto the other one and seek ourselves in him or her. In the moment we realize that the other one is different, we are disappointed and the crush is over just as quickly as it came.

Something like that probably happened in your relationship with Martin. You didn't really love him, but you were in love with being loved. Though you enjoyed his embraces and kisses, basically you were in love with yourself. This is why this phase is also called the autoerotic phase. *Autos* is the Greek word for "self." *Eros* is a Greek word for "love."

Masturbation is the physical expression of the autoerotic phase. When you masturbate you say: I am still immature. I am still in this first phase. (By the way, we would prefer to simply say m. from now on in our correspondence. This may be of help to you in case our correspondence falls in the hands of someone else.)

The autoerotic phase is followed by the homoerotic phase. *Homos* means "same." It refers to the time of the deep boy-to-boy and girl-to-girl friendships. This has nothing to do with homosexuality. It is healthy and necessary to pass through this phase. It is an in-between phase. On the one hand, we are able to direct our feelings to a "stranger," to someone who is not "myself," and yet we are not mature enough to direct them to a representative of the other sex. The purpose of these friendships is to learn how to handle love feelings without expressing them through sexual actions. To have such love feelings is normal. To transfer them into sexual activity is not normal.

This is why, at the moment, your girl friend is probably the most important person for you. You don't need to be afraid to hug and kiss each other. The more consciously you pass through the second phase, the sooner you will leave the first one and become better prepared for the third one.

In our day many young people jump over the second phase completely. Actually, as far as their attitude goes, they are still in the first phase, seeking and loving themselves although they enter into sexual activities which involve the other sex. Their feelings are not directed toward the other one, but they use the other one for their own satisfaction. Deep petting, which you call correctly a sort of mutual masturbation, is a typical expression of this situation. It is a heterosexual activity in an autoerotic attitude.

The danger is that a person remains somewhat in this autoerotic attitude even in marriage, and as a result he or she never reaches the maturity which is necessary for the encounter with the other sex, for entering the heteroerotic phase. (*Heteros* is the Greek word for "other," "different.")

Encounter with the other sex is difficult. It takes maturity to face the otherliness of the other one, to relate to someone who is so "strange," so different. Of course we are frightened by it, but it is a natural, normal fear. It takes maturity to overcome it. I believe that in our time the tendency to efface the differences between the sexes even in outward appearance is motivated by this fear. One feels inadequate to love someone who is different.

You participate in this fear when you are self-conscious around boys. It is a fear which corresponds with your present development. You are not yet able to overcome it, although probably because you have brothers you have it easier than girls who don't. For the present you must simply accept yourself with this self-consciousness, which is also a protection—and wait.

Somehow all three phases are to be found in you at the moment. The last one is beginning already to open up. You should now consciously enjoy the second one. You should gradually leave the first one behind. If you get dependent upon m. it means that you remain in the auto-erotic phase, and this can be called a "development failure." You grow from phase to phase by learning how to endure sexual tension without transferring it immediately into pleasure. The more you learn to stand up under tension, the more energy you set free in order to become mature.

This is an art, Ilona, and it takes work to learn it. This is what we meant when we said that we have to "work together." It takes work to develop will power, endurance and perseverance which you will need in order to overcome the childish and egotistical desire for pleasure. The goal is not to repress your desire or deny it as if it would not be there. No, you should admit to yourself, "I now have this desire." And then, consciously, you renounce the satisfaction of it in order to gain a much deeper satisfaction than you would have by giving in. Do you understand the difference between repressing and renouncing?

You ask where the inexplicable feeling of guilt comes from. (Strangely enough, non-Christians have it as well as Christians.) I think one reason is that deep down every person knows somehow that sexuality is given to us for the purpose of communication and that m. does not correspond to this purpose.

The other reason for the guilt feeling comes from an inner voice which says: You did have the possibility of standing up under tension—for example, when doing your homework—but you chose the cheap way out, the way of least resistance. This gives you the feeling of a cop-out, a defeat. The guilt feeling says: You hinder yourself in your own maturing process.

Giving up instead of giving in is the harder way. Giving up is also very much out of date. On the contrary, the tendency of our time is to consume, to gain pleasure, to reduce tension and to avoid suffering. This is why our time is so immature, so autistic and egocentric and why the relationships between the sexes have become such a problem both inside of and outside of marriage.

So we ask nothing less of you than to swim against the stream. We also know that in the final analysis nothing will help you but the certainty: I am able to renounce the satisfaction of a desire if I want to. I am no longer dependent upon it. Neither am I defenseless against the feeling of being stuck in a rut. I am no longer imprisoned by my ego.

You ask whether you can help Martin. You have helped him already by not pretending to have feelings which you do not have and by not playing with him. He has to learn how to live with the pain of lover's grief; this will make him grow.

Growth is very often connected with pain, Ilona. We wish you the strength to face this pain and not to run away from it. By the way growth and pain are a part of marriage also. To illustrate this fact we are sending you our book *I Married You*. If you know the goal, you can find the way.

November 11

Dear Mr. and Mrs. T.,

Thank you so much for your letter and especially for the book. It gave me a new vision for my own future marriage. What I liked best was the description of your own difficulties. I think I'm beginning to understand what you mean by "growing through pain" and the difficulties encountered through the "otherliness of the other one."

By the way, your last letter caused a small clash between my mother and me. She had of course noticed the package with the book and also your letters, and wanted to know what it was all about. Of course I could not tell her, and the tension that resulted was almost more than I could bear. It made me realize once again how dependent on my mother I still am.

Yes, I think you are probably correct that m. is partly defiance against my mother, an escape into something which belongs to me alone. It's really interesting that you mentioned cooking and baking in your letter. This is exactly what my mother never allowed me to do. At best I was accepted as her helper but never entrusted with any real responsibility.

Fortunately my mother did not open your letter. If she had, she would have certainly hit the ceiling and thought that I am not quite normal. (By the way, I still have difficulty with this term: Is m. normal or is it not? Please clarify.) Finally my father saved the situation, and I ended up having a good talk with both my parents. They understand now that I need to share my personal problems with someone outside of the family, and my mother suddenly remembered that she had done the same when she was my age.

My father was especially nice and even took me in his arms, all on his own accord! This assured me how much he loves me. Actually the distance between us has diminished, and there is even a positive side to it which I now see. Because he sees my everyday life through different eyes, it helps me to be more objective. Yes, he can be "strict" all right, but I like that. What do girls do who have no father?

What I have to tell you now is hard for me. For the first time since we began corresponding, m. has happened again. It was last Friday. I was so mad at myself that I repeated it three times. I did not even try to resist because I had no strength.

Yes, the difference between "repression" and "renunciation" makes sense to me. Renunciation stems from a completely different attitude. I can also understand that when I am able to renounce it and then give in anyway, guilt results.

But you would have to agree that there are also situations in which I am unable to renounce. The desire is so strong that I have no choice. If I would continue to resist, the tension would become unbearable and I would toss around all night. In such cases I think m. is necessary for release of tension.

I feel that the first reason you gave—that I don't use my sex drive for communication—is a better explanation for the guilt I feel. Your second reason—the inability to renounce—doesn't make me feel so guilty. Perhaps I am immature. Okay, I admit that. But is immaturity guilt? I feel that m. is then at least an honest expression of my immaturity. So in a way I feel guilty and not guilty at the same time. Do you follow me?

When I read your letter, I got the idea to read the tiger story again in your book *I Loved a Girl*.[9] I read it first a while ago, but I think that I understand its true meaning now for the first time.

When the keeper kept the tiger locked up because he was afraid of him, that was an act of "suppression," wasn't it? But then the tiger roared and gave no rest, and finally, in an unguarded moment, attacked. This is exactly what happens when the desire for m. possesses me.

However, when the keeper allowed the tiger to enter his most beautiful rooms and when he looked him straight in the eye without fear, the tiger became his friend and lay down at his feet.

As yet I have not succeeded in making friends with my sex drive. Therefore I am not yet able to master it and to renounce it.

But I would like to learn this, and as an attempt in that direction I have decided to give up m. until Christmas. I want to prove to myself that I am not dependent on it. I remember once that I made a similar promise to myself, and then was terribly disappointed when I broke it. But at that time I did not have your support. I want you to know how precious your support and encouragement is to me.

By the way, while reading *I Loved a Girl*, I came across the passage where you counsel Francois concerning m. and tell him to find new and fruitful channels for his desire. Do guys have the same difficulties with m. as girls?

No, sorry, I don't have a real hobby, and I'm not good in sports either. Formerly I enjoyed playing the flute. But because of school pressures, I gave it up. Since I finished my dance course, I have not danced either. I am a difficult case, am I not? But I am so thankful that I got to know you before it was too late. God seems to love me in spite of everything!

November 17

Dear Ilona,

We are glad that your parents understand that you want to correspond with us and that they respect your privacy. Children very rarely open up to their own parents with their intimate problems. It is wonderful that your father took you in his arms.

Yes, girls who grow up without a father or who have a cold, rather passive father certainly do find life more difficult. Very often they are looking for a substitute for the lack of fatherly tenderness in their relationship with a fellow. The young men, of course, misunderstand such a girl's need for tenderness and love, and think that all she wants is sex. This misunderstanding is often the reason for the "too-soon" sexual experiences. In any case, girls without a father are more tempted to premarital adventures. Needless to say such adventures end in disappointment every time because the girl does not find what she is looking for.

It is possible, however, to replace a father, to have a father-substitute, while it is almost impossible to replace a mother.

You ask about the word *normal*.[10] What we wanted to say is that m. is a typical behavior, which corresponds to the immature stage of the autoerotic phase. It is a typical expression of this phase but should not continue beyond it.

The word *normal* is not used here in the sense of a "required norm." Otherwise all those who do not masturbate would not be normal, and one estimates that at least forty per cent of all girls do not masturbate. They are, of course, as normal as all others.[11]

You ask about boys—whether they have the same difficulties. In general m. is more frequent among boys than among girls. The reason is that it is harder for boys to master their sex drive during the time of puberty. Mainly this is because of biological reasons and has to do with the hormones which the body begins to produce during this period of life. You see, no one is only man or only woman. Men have female hormones and women have male hormones. During puberty there is an almost equal balance of these hormones in the girl's body. Later on the female hormones get the upper hand and she becomes a young woman. But as long as the balance exists, male and female hormones could be said to "neutralize" each other. Therefore it is relatively easier for the girl to handle her sexual desires than it is for the boy during this period of development.[12]

With boys there is no such balance. The male hormones outnumber the female hormones considerably. Their sexual desire is therefore more impetuous and thus it may be more difficult for them to live in peace with it. This is why almost all boys pass through a period of masturbation, which they use as a means of releasing tension. They often discover it in connection with their so-called "wet dreams" at night, nature's way of taking care of the over-production of semen. It has been our experience that boys get started easier with masturbating, but it is also easier for them to stop.

Why this is we don't exactly know. One reason is certainly a physical one: A boy loses something when he masturbates, a precious substance of his body. He cannot do it repeatedly because for him there is a physical borderline. To do it three times in a row, as you wrote, is hardly possible for a boy. That is why the danger of becoming dependent upon it is relatively greater for a girl.

We can well understand what you mean by "honesty": the acceptance of your own immaturity which makes you think you must still masturbate. We would like to add that this "honesty" must also include the honest wish to outgrow this stage of immaturity which does not use the sex drive as it is meant to be used.

On the other hand, we think it is an excellent idea to distinguish between necessary and unnecessary m. The word "necessary" comes from the Latin word *ne*, which means "not," and *cedere* which means "to give way." Agreed, there may still be situations for you in which "m. does not give way," does not yield and when it becomes inevitable or "necessary." But you have honestly to admit that this is not always the case. There are certainly other situations when m. could give way and when it is avoidable. Our suggestion would be, for the time being, to set yourself a preliminary goal; in other words, to avoid m. when it is avoidable.

If the pressure is unbearable and you indeed have "no

choice," all right. Then, in this stage of your development, you may have to be "honestly immature" and give in. However, if actually there is no sexual pressure and if it is only a cowardly escape from a disliked activity, then it is certainly avoidable and you have no excuse to give in. If you succeed in refraining from m. when it is not really necessary and when it is avoidable because there are other ways of dealing with these feelings of frustration, we think that you will soon get the good feeling of making progress.

Only you can judge when m. is avoidable and when it is not. We are not your judges. It is very difficult to give any general rules about dealing with m. because sexual pressure is for some people stronger than for others. Some, including many girls, would say that they do not even know situations where m. would be necessary. Others may need this emergency release more often or for a longer period of time. This is why one has to deal with each person differently and in a way you have to become your own "therapist."

May we ask you, How did you yourself feel about your experience of last Friday?

Yes, Ilona, God loves you. Unconditionally and without limit. You have to cling to this fact without doubting. We are happy if our letters can become for you a small outward sign of this love. But in the final analysis you stand alone before God in this experience of being loved, exactly as you stand alone before God in the experience of being guilty. He alone is judge. It is up to you, not up to us, to decide when and whether you have become guilty before the God who loves you.

November 24

Dear Mrs. T.,

Today I want to write to you personally because it is easier for me to write to a woman about something very intimate.

First of all, thank you for the preliminary goal you set for me. I know that it's only a step toward the ultimate goal, but having in sight a mile stone that can be reached helps reduce my fear of being overcome by the compulsion to give in to m. I know now: I *may* give in, if it is really necessary. I am sure that this knowledge alone and the freedom from fear will help tremendously to diminish m's grip on me. I also realize that the crutch of this permission does not yet represent the final stage of maturity, but at least it helps me relax a bit and not be so apprehensive.

Therefore again: Thank you that for the time being I only have to work on eliminating the avoidable, unnecessary m.

In retrospect I would analyze my behavior on that Friday as follows: I was mad at m. because it was dominating me—and I was mad at myself that I would allow myself to be so enslaved. I could have slapped my face! And I did by repeating m. I punished the tiger in myself and myself in the tiger. That's the way I see it now.

I realize that the repetition was absolutely unnecessary,

and I am ashamed of it before God. In that moment, however, it was as if I were possessed. This makes me very much aware of how closely I walk along the abyss of dependency, yes, almost to the point of addiction, and how quickly I relapse into that state.

Therefore I can only be relieved and thankful that since that Friday when I did it so often, m. has not happened again. And that was already three weeks ago! Since summer vacation I haven't been able to go for such a long period of time without m. The temptation is still there, but somehow I have the strength not to give in, and I am even able to resist the temptation to tell myself that it is "necessary" when it really isn't.

After a hard test the other day, I "rewarded" myself in the afternoon. Not by m. as I would formerly have done, but by something better: I read a book which I had been burning to read for mere pleasure and entertainment. Result: The avoidable m. was avoided.

But now to my question: Recently I had a dream about m. I woke up and realized that I had to go to the toilet. I remember distinctly now that when I was thirteen or fourteen I discovered that when I held back my urine, a very pleasant sensation resulted. It is the same now. Is there a connection?

And something else: Sometimes I sort of envy boys who, to put it quite frankly, are able to play with their penis. Do you understand what I mean? To accept my own sexuality, the specifics of my gender, is for me still an unfinished task.

There is also an aching question I have about what it

November 27

Dear Ilona,

Your good letter—from woman to woman —arrived yesterday. Since I have to leave on a trip tomorrow I want to answer it right away. Otherwise you might have to wait for some time.

First of all, I'd like to congratulate you on getting along without m. for such a long time. Also that you thought in a creative way of a reward. By the way, I doubt that m. is ever "necessary" in the deepest sense of the word. It may be an in-between solution which helps release pressure and reduce tension, but I think it is much more "necessary" to learn how to stand up under pressure and how to live with tension.

There we are again on our topic of becoming mature and becoming a woman. It is just this which is "necessary" —not m. In this context it might be helpful for you if you start living consciously with your cycle.

Now to answer your questions: Yes, there is a connection between that band of muscle which holds back the urine and the sexual pleasure which a woman feels in the vagina.

This muscle is called the pubococcygeus muscle. The nerve endings in the muscle reach the vagina. If this muscle is weak and under-developed, it can be a reason

why some women have difficulty finding sexual fulfillment in marriage. I have explained this in detail in my
book *The Joy of Being a Woman*. I only wish that many
girls would read this book before marriage.[13]

But before you can become a wife, you have to become
a woman. You can become a woman without becoming a
wife, but not the other way around. Yes, if you know the
goal, you can find the way. Your first goal therefore is to
become a woman, not to get married. You don't even
know yet whether you will get married some day. This is an
open question. But the goal of becoming a woman you
must reach in any case.

The first goal is to accept yourself as a young woman
and to live your gender. I agree with you that there is still
something lacking at this point. It is interesting to me that in
the snapshot of yourself you sent me in order for me to
"picture" you better you are wearing jeans.

I have nothing against pants. I like to wear them myself
and in many ways they are more practical than skirts and
certainly warmer in cold weather. But if you feel more
"yourself" when wearing pants, I wonder whether it could
be an expression of the fact that you have not yet completely accepted yourself as a woman. Be honest—
wouldn't you sometimes really prefer to be a boy?

This leads us to the "penis envy" you spoke of in your
letter. Here too you are very "normal." Sigmund Freud
built a whole theory about the development of female
sexuality upon this envy. I certainly don't believe today
that it is as important as he was led to believe it was fifty
and more years ago. However, there is some truth in it.

The day will come, Ilona, when you will realize that you do not have something less than a man so that you feel inferior, deprived or "castrated." On the contrary, you have something more: the possibility of a sexual experience which the man does not have.

This brings us back to the pubococcygeus muscle. Indeed there is a strange connection between this muscle and the self-acceptance of a woman. As long as your "beautiful feeling" is related to the clitoris alone, you are actually still in the area of a masculine experience of sexual pleasure. Physically speaking, the clitoris resembles the penis, though much smaller, and it would have become a penis had you been born a boy. Seeing it from this point of view, m. could be a sign that you have not yet fully accepted your gender. If m. becomes a habit, self-acceptance as a woman will become more and more difficult.

In comparison with a man, a woman's sexual feeling in the vagina is richer and more fulfilling. You must believe me, even though you cannot yet experience it. It is an experience which basically can take place only in the shelteredness of a good marriage as one of the fruits of mutual trust and love with the partner to whom one is united for life.

Personally I feel strongly that it is one of the privileges of womanhood to be able to carry and give birth to a child. My life has certainly not become poorer, but infinitely richer, through these children.

You think that the routine of a housewife is dull and monotonous. It depends on how you look at it. I feel it takes all the qualities of a superexecutive to face up to the

51

challenge of being a wife and mother. It calls for every bit of creativity she can muster. Perhaps because I had a very satisfying career before marriage, I see it differently than a woman who has not had this experience. I can only say that never have I felt more fulfilled than when I could fulfill the needs of my husband and children.

I don't think that you love yourself too much, Ilona. Rather I don't think you love yourself enough.

I must close now in order to prepare for my trip tomorrow. If you write during my absence, my husband will answer your letter.

November 27

Dear Mr. and Mrs. T.,

Sorry. M. has happened again. I gave in again, just when I was so happy that I had seemingly overcome it. I guess I was just too sure of myself. I thought I had defeated the tiger, and I neglected to keep my eyes on him.

Since I went to bed very late last night, I decided to take a nap today after lunch. I should not have done that, because shortly before I fell asleep I already sensed that m. was hanging in the air. Then when the alarm clock rang, it indeed happened again.

And I had done so well during the last three weeks! I had really experienced the strength to overcome m., and I am sure that this strength was from God. But when the actual moment of temptation came, where was this strength?

I don't know where to go from here. I am just where I was at the beginning. I broke my promise to wait until Christmas. Can I really begin again after all that? I am afraid that I shall never be rid of m.

I am writing you this letter immediately after it happened and I shall mail it right away. I would like to do the same in the future. Forcing myself to write it to you may help me to stop. Will you permit me to use you as a "dumping place"? I shall feel unburdened when this letter is in the mail box.

I did not dare to mail this letter yesterday. I was too ashamed—and still am. What will you answer me?

You will probably ask me whether m. was avoidable or not. To be honest, I must say yes. It could have been avoided had I gotten up immediately after my nap. But at that moment I simply did not want to renounce m.

I must admit that I always feel guilty afterwards, even if it was "necessary." But I don't remind myself of that beforehand. No, before it happens I don't think about feeling guilty.

Is m. a sin? Do I have to repent for m.? In which way does one repent? In your letter of November 17, you said that it is up to me to judge whether or not I am guilty when I give in to m. But I am not sure. I can't say one way or the other.

I am forcing myself now to send this letter.

November 29

Dear Ilona,

Don't be sad! I'm not at all surprised that you were not able to keep your promise. As for me, I would never have asked for such a promise from you, because the attempt to set a time limit usually fails. But it was your own idea and I didn't want to suggest otherwise. I wanted you to try.

The length of the intervals between your experiences of m. must develop more or less naturally, without chin-ups or forced effort. You should rejoice in the progress you have made instead of concentrating on your failures.

I would like to repeat, Ilona, you *may* masturbate as long as it is necessary. There is no reason why you should be afraid—afraid of m., afraid of my reaction, afraid that you will never become free from it. Fear is your greatest enemy. Remember the example of looking into the headlights of the car at night?

It is a little bit like skiing. You certainly are allowed to fall down. In fact it is a part of the learning process until the skier masters the slope. Of course no one aims to fall down and it is to be avoided if possible. But one knows: I *may* fall if it is necessary. The less the fear of falling, the less likely it is to happen.

If, in spite of everything, a good skier can't help falling

down, he doesn't take it too seriously. He doesn't sit in the snow, feeling sorry for himself and becoming depressed. Rather, he gets up, brushes himself off and continues on his way. The next time he takes the slope, he will try to do it without falling down. If, however, the skier throws himself into the snow on purpose three times in a row just because he's angry and frustrated that he fell down in the first place and to prove he can't ski and will never learn, then he becomes guilty for he impedes growth.

This brings us to your difficult question concerning guilt. For the first time in your letters, you used the word *sin*. I have avoided it purposely up until now, because sin means more than guilt. It opens up a new dimension—that of man's relationship to God. A person who doesn't believe in God can still feel guilty before others and himself. But sin implies guilt before God. When you ask whether m. is a sin, you are asking whether m. disturbs the personal relationship between a person and God.

I would like to share something with you which has become clear to me, not only through our correspondence but through my reading and correspondence with others: M. seems to take a unique place when it comes to sexual behavior—unique in three respects.

First, one can talk and write about almost anything today without anyone being embarrassed or feeling uncomfortable: about adultery, extramarital or premarital sex, abortion, homosexuality and every conceivable perversion. Some may even boast about participating in such activities. But a peculiar veil of embarrassment, uneasiness and uncomfortableness is spread over the subject of masturbation.

Second, and I believe I have already mentioned this, masturbation is the only sexual behavior as far as girls are concerned (and probably also for boys) that is affected by the mother-child relationship.

Third, recent studies in America have called attention to the fact that no other sexual behavior is so closely connected with a person's religion and relationship to God.[14] The feeling of guilt that appears after the act has been done, although it wasn't present beforehand, simply cannot be explained on a rational, purely psychological basis. A voice from an outside source speaks.

"Where do I find strength in such a moment?" you ask. The strength lies in the ability to hear this voice and to recognize the tiger ready to spring when m. is "hanging in the air." This takes practice, however. The more you mature, the more you will acquire this ability; the more you acquire this ability, the more you will mature.

December 1

Dear Mr. T.,

Thank you so much for the "ski letter" and also that you wrote immediately. Your letter comforted me and was a challenge at the same time. It means that I have to decide myself whether m. is sin for me—or at least whether it is always sin for me. Yet I am still unable to do so.

In the meantime your wife's letter of November 27 arrived, crossing with my "ski accident" letter of the same day. Her letter confused me completely and made me reconsider whether or not I really want to give up m. I feel that I simply must write you immediately concerning my doubts and confusion.

In a way your wife's letter could also be an answer to my question concerning guilt. If one continues to follow a path even though he knows that it will not lead to the desired destination, one certainly becomes guilty. Of course, "If one knows the goal, one can find the way." Or to put it in my own words, "Unless one is sure of the destination, he is unable to choose the route to get there."

And this is where my problem comes: Since I read your wife's letter, I am no longer sure of my destination. Marriage does not appeal to me as such an attractive goal as your wife describes it.

My parents do love each other, but the example of marriage they have given me is rather sad. If I found marriage to be an attractive and worthwhile goal for my life, everything would be easier and I would have the strength and will power to give up m. But this is not the case, and therefore I vacillate between this distant and questionable goal and my sex drive.

Even if marriage is as beautiful as your wife describes it, the question torments me: What does that mean then if I never do get married?

If I knew for sure that I would someday marry, it would be easier to renounce m. for the present in anticipation of something better later on. But what if there is no "later on"?

Suppose I become a nun or join a community of unmarried women or for any other reason never get married: What will happen to my sexuality? How can I sacrifice something for a future which may possibly never come? Do you understand what I mean?

Your wife herself advised me not to set marriage as my exclusive and ultimate goal. That means that my renunciation may not only be temporary but permanent. The thought of "forever" simply drains me. It's not that I lack the strength to resist but that I simply lack the desire.

I tell myself, "Even though m. is only a poor substitute for the real thing, it is at least something—especially considering the possibility that I may never experience the real thing, the "fulfillment" your wife speaks about. I know good and well that the meaning of life is greater than sexuality—and still I cannot deny these thoughts. They are there and I have to face them.

If becoming a woman is supposed to be my goal, is it possible to become a woman without practicing sex? Yes, now I have it—this is indeed my basic and crucial question.

I thank you in advance for the answer you will send me. I hope it will be an answer which not only enables me to give up m. but which also makes me willing to give it up.

I must tell you frankly that I just did it again today, intentionally and rather defiantly. I am not willing to give it up, and I did not want to repress it. I am being completely honest with you.

And yet it is strange: I did it consciously, willingly and without any guilt feelings. Nevertheless I have to admit that I am not at peace with myself. It is exactly as you described it—unexplainable.

The only plausible explanation seems to be that m. for me is an expression of the fact that I have not yet fully accepted myself. Your wife is right— I have a problem with self-acceptance. This thought preoccupies my mind more and more.

However, as far as self-love is concerned, your wife's letter confused me here also. In your first letter you wrote that I should not rotate so much around my own self, and later on you challenged me to outgrow the autoerotic phase. Now your wife writes that I don't love myself enough. Do I love myself too much or too little? Is m. a symptom of one or the other? And what does your wife mean when she says that I should learn "to live consciously with my cycle"?

Sorry that this has become such a problematic letter . .

December 13

Dear Ilona,

So you have fallen short of your goal! I am thankful that you have spoken so openly, but at the same time I rather dread answering your letter. You ask very difficult questions that deal with the basic fabric of life. There are no easy answers.

Just suppose for a moment that you will never marry. Does that mean you must deny your sexuality your whole life long? The answer is NO. This is impossible to do because your sexuality is you. You are your sexuality. That which you have to renounce is not your sexuality but only one form of its expression—the genital expression.

Can you still be a woman without this specific form of expression? The answer is YES. Let us go back to your example of nuns or a community of unmarried women. In their lives too their sexuality is a part of their being. Single people are able to radiate a special quality of sexuality when they have learned to be fulfilled men and women—maybe just because they have renounced its genital expression.

Becoming mature, becoming complete men and women, is therefore the goal for unmarried people as well. *Unmarried* often has a negative connotation, implying an unfulfilled state. That's why I prefer the word *single*, which carries with it a sense of "freedom." Single people are free from being bound to someone else, free from being dependent upon a mate, free from marriage and the restrictions it brings. *Unmarried* then has the positive meaning of "unrestricted."

Married people, on the other hand, are "unfree" in the sense that they are tied down to their spouse and family. Try to look at singleness from this angle too. Maybe then you will not be so frightened of it.

The responsibility of becoming complete men and women belongs to married and single people alike. When a single woman has achieved this goal, then she can pour out her whole self—her femininity, her motherliness, her ability to devote herself to others (in other words, her sexuality)—into her work and calling. The fulfillment which she receives from doing this would cause her to burst out laughing if someone were to suggest that perhaps she should masturbate so that she would "at least have something." She has so channeled her sexuality into serving others that the renouncing of its genital expression is no effort for her but is experienced as a gift and joy.

In order for you to better understand what I mean, may I remind you of something we have already written you? Sexuality is language, it is communication, it is relationship; it reaches out its hand, it seeks to touch other's lives, it is ready to give. That is its meaning and that is what makes sexuality human.

The single person may also learn its language, although he or she will choose another vocabulary to express this language than the married person. Through m., however, sexuality misses its target. Basically that is why m. is an unworthy or inhuman expression of sexuality and precisely not "at least something." It divides a person in two, for he must play two incompatible roles simultaneously—that of the stimulus giver and stimulus receiver.[15]

M. is not language, it is silence—mute isolation. No communication, no relationship emerges from it. The person speaks to no one and gives to no one; he only takes something for himself.

There is no gain in this form of taking. The person takes something for himself which he desires and fears will be withheld from him. It is just by doing this though that he takes something *from* himself; he loses something, namely the ability to give himself to another.

Renouncing something may be difficult if you think of not getting something you want. But is it so difficult to renounce losing something, depriving yourself of something?

Once you can say to yourself: I am able to renounce, I can give up depriving myself, I no longer have to live under the compulsion of continually taking away something from myself—then you will discover a new inner joy and sense of freedom.

Ilona, I really want to help you gain this inner joy. I am wondering if we could not find another "training ground" for practicing "renouncement." The Bible calls renouncing *fasting*. A person fasts from something that is allowed, not from something that is forbidden. In renouncing the allowable, you acquire the ability to renounce the forbidden. Is there some area in your life in which you would be

65

willing to "hold a fast"?

In your first letter you mentioned your eating habits. Overeating, as well as smoking, often may be a substitute form of masturbation. Here is the connection: You eat in order to fill a love need. But you would be happier if you ate less. The same is true with m. You try to love yourself through m., but you would love yourself more without m.

You ask whether you love yourself too much or too little? I think you do both at the same time. We must distinguish here between two different forms of self-love. One type of self-love is self-centered and egotistic. The other form of self-love is found in the person who has accepted himself, found himself, and therefore is able to let go of himself and give himself to others. The first type of self-love is innate, but the second type of self-love must be acquired. It is this type of self-love that Jesus referred to when he said, "Love your neighbor *as yourself.*"[16]

I would say that you love yourself too much when you think of the first type of self-love and not enough when you think of the second type. Both are evident through m.

When my wife wrote that "you should live in harmony with your cycle," she was trying to help you develop this second type of self-love; the love and acceptance of yourself as a woman. This is your goal. But she can explain better herself what she means by this statement. She will return home tomorrow.

For today, I'd just like to add this word: Start all over again, Ilona, and don't give up!

December 15

Dear Ilona,

I have just returned from my trip and I would like to answer your question right away. When I suggested that you learn to live more in harmony with your menstrual cycle, I meant that you should be aware of the process of ovulation.

Perhaps you have noticed that on certain days of the month you have a feeling of wetness at the vaginal opening. This is called cervical mucus and has nothing to do with menstrual bleeding since it begins usually a few days after menstruation. It is a sign that the time of ovulation is approaching and lasts mostly from four to six days. As it becomes more plentiful, it also becomes stretchy and clear in appearance, much like raw egg white. Some women also experience a sharp pain in the lower abdomen around the time of ovulation. It is also possible to pinpoint the time of ovulation by taking your waking temperature every morning. After ovulation, that is, after the ovum has left the ovary (usually 12-14 days *before* the next menstruation) the basal body temperature rises a little and remains on this higher level until shortly before menstruation.[17]

You may realize that your mood changes after ovulation has taken place. Women are often more optimistic and "together" in the first part of the cycle, while in the second part they may become more easily discouraged and "down." You may also observe that your sexual desire is stronger perhaps just before menstruation. Then you can be inwardly prepared and the "tiger" cannot easily overcome you.

The knowledge of the cycle is indispensable for marriage and one of its best preparations. But even if you don't get married, this self-observance is a decisive help in learning self-acceptance and the right kind of self-love. This is why I believe that girls should begin in their teens "to live consciously with their cycle."

I hope you are satisfied with my husband's answers to your difficult questions. I am glad he answered them, for I know I couldn't have done it that well. You see, there is sometimes an advantage also in not being single. . . .

God wants to start anew with you—and that is why you also can start anew.

I'm praying for you, Ilona.

Easter

Dear Mr. and Mrs. T.,

Four months have passed since I wrote you last. Your last letter was a decisive help for me. Thank you for setting me straight again. My goal is again clear.

After I read your last letter, I sat down quietly and did some thinking about myself. I said to myself, "You are not a little girl anymore. And you want to become a young woman. There must be a way to achieve this goal." Now I understand why, from the very beginning, you did not address me as a child, but as an adult. You talked to the adult in me, and this helped me to regain my self-respect.

I came to the following conclusion: As long as I am dependent upon m. it is, without any doubt, a sin for me.

It was a happy coincidence that on the same afternoon I had to prepare a Christmas devotion about the following verse:

He has anointed me to preach the Good News to the poor,

He has sent me to proclaim liberty to the captives,

And recovery of sight to the blind,

To set free the oppressed,

To announce the year when the Lord will save his people.

(Luke 4:18-19, *Good News for Modern Man*)

When I tried to apply this verse to my own life, it was as if scales fell from my eyes, and it suddenly struck me how I myself am a captive. If I wish to tell others that Jesus can help us concretely in our everyday life, then I must also expect him to reach down and help me in my own specific situation and captivity. Again my goal was clear.

On the same afternoon a book fell into my hand with the title *Ten Great Freedoms*. In this book the author, Ernst Lange, commented on the commandment, "You shall not commit adultery." He said, "You don't need to indulge sexually—either by telling dirty stories, daydreaming and fantasizing, masturbating, or by abusing others for your own satisfaction. Don't deprive yourself of the joys of real love through the handling of the counterfeits of love. I, the almighty God, am the author of true happiness, and I desire only the best for you. You can afford to wait for the partner whom I shall send you."[18]

Thinking of your letter, I added in my heart, "You can afford to allow yourself time to grow into full womanhood."

On that afternoon God spoke to me as clearly as if we were standing face to face. But I did not repeat my mistake of setting an unrealistic goal again. I knew that if m. was absolutely necessary, I was allowed to do it. That reduced my fear and anxiety. Therefore, since November 27, it has not happened even once. Today, it is really Easter for me!

In the meantime, I have graduated from high school. The concentrated studies for my finals was also a help for me. Besides that, I made use of the other helps which you suggested—renunciation and self-observation.

In order to practice what it means to renounce, I decided voluntarily to give up eating sweets, except for dessert when I was invited for dinner and felt it would be impolite to refuse. When I received sweets as a present, I gave them to someone else. It was really difficult, but it helped me to learn a basic attitude which has helped in controlling m.

Whether there is a connection between m. and my menstrual cycle, I am unable to say for sure. I believe that the last two times m. happened, it was eight or nine days before menstruation. It is not even necessary for me to take my temperature to discern when I ovulate. I am able to tell from the other symptoms such as the cervical mucus and the midpain. I am keeping records and have started to live in harmony with my sexuality instead of fighting it.

Finally I want to tell you about my friendship with Arndt. He is twenty-three and from Amsterdam. We met during a special course and seemed to like each other from the very beginning. We had many good, open talks about spiritual problems and also about our relationship. We agreed from the beginning to keep the physical expression to a minimum.

On the last day, however, we kissed in spite of this. I guess the pain of separation was the main motive. I told him frankly that I could not fully back up this action with my feelings for him. We decided to continue our relationship in such frankness with each other and before God.

By the way, Martin suddenly appeared the other day on my doorstep and asked how I was doing. He caught me by surprise indeed. I still remember how disappointed I was when I broke up with him and he completely accepted it without even trying to object. Now I am equally surprised to see him again. How should I interpret this? How should I react now that Arndt is also in the picture? I am so unsure of myself in such matters. Maybe it is because I went to a girls' school. . . .

And now something stupid: I sometimes worry that I might lose you when m. is overcome. May I continue to write to you anyway?

May 5

Dear Ilona,

I don't think we need to say how happy we were to receive your letter. We must admit we were rather uneasy because you had not written to us for such a long time. On the other hand, we felt that we should not impose ourselves upon you and so we quietly endured this time of silence. That is why your letter made us doubly thankful, and we can sense the joy which you feel. You have taken a giant step forward, Ilona. You have found yourself. As Søren Kierkegaard says, "The way to yourself is the most difficult way of all."

No, you will not lose us. We are united with each other by more than just this problem. We have reflected a lot about your decision to sit down, meditate and then consciously assert your will as an ally in your struggle. We think that in our day, will power is made use of much too seldom and that the will is underestimated as a force in resistance.[19]

The simplest explanation for Martin's visit to you is that he is a young man. At his age neither a declaration of love or a decision to give up a girl are as deeply rooted for him as they would be for a girl. You shouldn't attach too much importance to his visit, but neither should you underrate it. Our advice would be for you simply to keep in contact with him on a friendly, natural basis, but at the same time let him know that you have other fellows as friends. This includes Arndt.

What you say about your girls' school is certainly right. But there is also a positive side to it. Often the process of growth and maturity is not hindered as much as in a co-educational school when the fire of a love relationship can be experienced too early.

As you know, we lived in Africa for many years. During our years in the savannah where there were only a few scattered trees, we often wondered why the trees grew so crooked. Rarely did we see a straight tree trunk. We discovered that the reason for this is that every year during the dry season grass fires are lit in order to clear the ground. Of course this disturbed the growth of the trees year by year. You have been spared such disturbances in your life.

We are very happy to hear that you can live consciously with your cycle. You will see that this is certainly a great help in growing up straight.

June 10

Dear Mr. and Mrs. T.,

How right you were concerning Martin! Everything is just as you felt it would be. He called me up once, and then last Sunday he made a formal farewell visit. But this was meant for the whole family.

My correspondence with Arndt continues to be good. We have discovered many things we have in common. But we don't know yet where it is going to lead us. The next step we see is simply that we try to get to know each other better through corresponding and hopefully by meeting each other again one day.

One thing has confused me, however. Arndt wrote that when he thinks about me, his sexual tension increases to the point where he has to masturbate in order to find release. Well, I was a little bit shocked that he shared that with me, also considering that he touched on my problem, without knowing it of course. On the other hand I was happy that he had so much confidence in me to speak openly. How should I react? Can I, as a girl, help him with his problem? I decided not to react at all for the time being.

This brings up the topic of m. again. I have another very important question about it (I hope that this is the last one!) First of all, I am really happy that I am not dependent anymore upon m., that I am no longer a captive. And

I want to thank you again for your patience with me and your understanding.

But now to my question: At the beginning of this week, I suddenly felt such a joy about my body as I have never felt before. I think that I am succeeding more and more in accepting my sexuality, not only mentally but with my feelings too. In this state of mind the desire for m. returned. It came from a completely different source than formerly. It wasn't a surprise attack from outside but a deep longing from inside.

Is it possible that my "beautiful feeling" can also be an expression of the joy I feel about my own body? Or would I just cheat myself and become a captive again?

Yes, I was able to resist. I have learned this by now. But there is still the nagging question: Is m. always sin?

It was and is clear for me that m. is sin for me as long as I am captive to it. But if I am not any longer captive? If I am free? Do I have the liberty to grant myself this beautiful feeling—to "treat myself" to it as to a nice trip, a visit to the theater or a dinner by candlelight? To be sure, it would be rarely—only as something very special. I don't think that that would necessarily have to result in dependence and captivity.

I admit that it would still not be using the gift of sex as a form of communication or expression of deep commitment to another person. I also admit that it would be a superficial experience and remain on the surface. But does one always have to live like a frogman diving into deep water?

Please, don't get angry about these questions! But if

you are, then please include this next question under your reasons to be angry. You wrote once that you also correspond with others about m. Am I being too intrusive to ask how others solve the problem? Do they also suffer from daydreams with sexual fantasies? Why doesn't God deliver me from them?

I remember a dream I had one night. I dreamt that I was a man and that I was about to marry my girl friend. Just as we went to pick up the marriage license, I saw my first boyfriend whom I knew from dance school. Suddenly I was a girl again, and I leaned happily against him.

What is going on inside of me? Around this same time I had a deep longing for a boy friend or a girl friend who would really understand me. Perhaps that had some influence on my dream.

Dear Ilona,

No, we certainly are not angry or annoyed by your questions. Instead we feel rather helpless. Regardless of what we answer to your question, it could be wrong. If we say no absolutely and thus deny you the liberty of a special gratification to yourself, then we put you under the law and this we have tried to avoid from the beginning. If we say yes and give you a green light, then it's like telling you to walk on a tightrope where you risk falling down.

We have talked about your letter for a long time. To be honest, it's the first time we are not completely in agreement. Ingrid tends, for love's sake, to say no. She thinks the danger of self-deception is too great. She also cannot imagine that m. would be as "beautiful" as say, a trip, a concert or a dinner by candlelight.

As for me, I would be ready, also for love's sake, to give a more daring answer. I would trust you to discern between a harmless gratification and becoming captive to something which also could disturb your relationship to God. Ingrid feels that this would be putting too great a burden on you, and since she feels this strongly as a woman, I don't want to argue her point.

Your question concerning experiences which others

have made is certainly justified. Thinking of those who have shared with us this problem, I must admit that Ingrid is right. Most of them were unable to make the distinction mentioned above. We are willing to confide to you some ways by which others have handled this problem. However, you must promise us not simply to transfer this to yourself. The main difficulty in finding a solution applicable to everyone is—and I think we have mentioned this already—that sexual pressure is simply different with different people. For some it is easier and for others it is harder to master their sex drive. Also the same person may find it easier or harder depending upon different situations and different stages of life. Those who find it harder are certainly not inferior people, let alone inferior Christians.

The only general experience which we have observed is that no one is really happy with m., even those who think of it as something harmless or even positive. Not only are most of them unhappy, but they also suffer.

We know people who became free completely through the experience of confession and absolution and through a new surrender to Christ. From that day on m. belonged for them to the past.

Others we know whom God guided patiently through a longer way of gradual overcoming. We think, for example, of a twenty-two-year-old girl, for whom m. had become a habit ever since childhood so that she was unable to fall asleep without it. She had to take it like a sleeping pill and suffered very much, repeating it sometimes even during the day.

It would not have helped her if we had tried to convince

her that there was nothing wrong with it. She felt base, inferior and dirty. We worked first of all with her on the prolongation of the intervals while at the same time we tackled her problem of loneliness. When she could abstain from it every other day, she got the feeling that she was making progress. Gradually it became more and more infrequent and today she is completely free from it. But it took almost a year.

If we had promised her at the beginning that Christ would set her free from one day to the next, she probably would have come into a severe spiritual crisis. After a defeat she should have concluded: Even Christ does not help me; therefore there is no hope for me.

Of course she had to fight also with her fantasies. We advised her not to deny these thoughts and suppress them —not to put the tiger in the cellar, for then he roars at night. If you try to throw these imaginations out the front door, then they come back in again through the back door. We told her to simply admit to herself that she had these thoughts and then learn to accept herself *with* them—to say to herself: I am a person who has such ideas. This was for her the first step toward healing.

During a certain period of time it also helped her to jot the thoughts and imagined scenes down on a piece of paper so that they were not any more within her, but she could look at them objectively outside of her. She burned the notes afterwards or put them in an envelope and mailed them to us so that they were disposed of. At first this happened almost daily, but after a while it ceased completely.

Today she is not entirely free from such fantasies—no one is—but she does not feel threatened by them anymore. She has learned to smile at them—scornfully and disdainfully—and in this way they have lost their power over her.

There is one thing that the devil can't stand, Ilona, and that is humor. As long as we take our problems so deadly serious, we become an easy prey for him.

The real danger of fantasizing is that it may become a necessity in order to get "turned on." Later on in marriage one may be unable then to really encounter one's partner because his reality does not correspond with these fantasies. Also our imaginations may drive us into action against our better judgment.[20]

We are enclosing an article by Mary Stewart, an American psychologist. It might interest you because she also shares her personal experiences with fantasies.[21]

We wonder whether this article might also help Arndt. It was certainly wise not to react when he shared his problems with you. No, at your age, you definitely cannot help a fellow with this problem. It is also very difficult to help someone spiritually in depth when you are in love with that person. You could ask him if he would like to write to us, but in no case should you share your own struggles in the sexual realm with him. We think that if you simply keep silent, he will sense that he has overstepped the borderline beyond which sharing is unwholesome—at least in the present stage of your relationship.

Your dream means simply that there is still an overlapping of the homoerotic and the heteroerotic phases and that you still are in search of your own identity as a girl. Both of us doubt very much whether allowing yourself m. would help you in this search.

But now let us take another case. A young man training for a business career was a passionate cello player. When he had to prepare for his final exams, he decided to give up his daily cello playing. At the same time he started to masturbate. We told him simply to start playing his cello again and m. stopped immediately.

Another boy fought valiantly, but on rare occasions he had to give in. Because of these few times he felt condemned, perverse and dirty, and he tortured himself with self-reproaches. In this case I told him, "Just do it if you have to. You are neither condemned, nor perverse nor dirty because of it." Years later he wrote to me that after I had told him that he never did it again. It had lost the attraction of things forbidden. Of course we might not have given this advice to someone else because this same advice could have been completely wrong to someone in a different situation.

Another young man, a Christian, called m. the "smaller evil" and justified it as a protection for his fiancée and their relationship to each other. We did not contradict him. In his last letter he said that this form of release became less and less necessary the more his love for his fiancée grew.

Widows, above all young widows, are in a class by themselves. It is especially hard for them to live in peace with their sexuality because it is fully awakened, and they are still attached with their whole heart to their beloved spouse. Sometimes it is a help for them to allow m. once during a cycle when the pressure is especially strong. This is usually the case just before menstruation. They do not think that this is an ideal solution, but it helps them to live without fear and in peace with themselves. For them it is not simply an autoerotic act because they think of their deceased husband. Again this is not the solution for everyone.

Recently a seventy-year-old widow wrote to us: "After the death of my husband I frequently had erotic dreams which sometimes caused such tension that I had pain. My gynecologist advised me to masturbate. I told her that for me m. would be sin or at least something which destroys my self-respect. She replied that I should think of the many women who are forced to live singly all their lives. This statement on her part made my opinion a little shaky."

We could only answer her that we know people who are neither bothered in their conscience nor in their relationship to God when they achieve release by m. as an emergency measure. We do not judge these people and accept the fact that they may have this liberty before God. Without any doubt this emergency masturbation is something different than a regular habit or an addiction-like dependency. It is also something different from what you speak of when you "allow yourself a gratification."

We also know people who simply declare that every time they give in to m. their relationship to God is destroyed, even if they do it in an emergency situation. For them the only help is a personal assurance of forgiveness and a new beginning in God's strength.

You see, Ilona, how difficult the answer to your question is. Everyone has to decide here for himself. No one is allowed to judge the other one and no one can decide for him. If you want to walk on the tightrope, you have to take the responsibility for yourself. We are not the lords of your conscience. It is the Holy Spirit who alone has to tell you in each situation whether you can have a good conscience or not.

We walk beside you with trepidation, but we let you go, prayerfully, into the freedom of maturity.

July 15

Dear Mr. and Mrs. T.,

I wish your last letter could have been the last one you had to send me. What a glorious conclusion to our correspondence! Ilona, the valiant and pious, has solved her problem! She can at last be released into the "freedom of maturity."

Oh no, she cannot!

I have just produced myself the best evidence that m. is and always will be sin for me. Yesterday afternoon it happened again—twice or even three times. No doubt you will be shocked and disappointed when I tell you that I don't even know anymore how often it happened.

Well, when I sat down this afternoon to think about it, all I could remember about yesterday was the terrific emotional rebellion I felt. Using psychological terms, you would probably call it "feelings of aggression." I've been trying to analyze them to get to the root of the problem. *Why* did I backslide?

On the surface there are several things that could account for it. Pressure from school made me realize that I had a lot of studying to do, and I was frustrated that I could not quickly grasp what I had to learn and that studying was so difficult for me.

Besides that, I felt a certain conflict of interests: My

mother was outside working in the garden, and I wanted to help her because I knew it was too much for her. On the other hand, I had to study if I did not want to fall behind in my courses and receive bad marks.

Studying at the university is so new for me and so different from what I am used to. In high school I knew all the teachers, their individual methods of testing and grading, and I felt "at home" in the system. Now I find it difficult to develop a new style of studying where I am completely responsible for organizing my time and keeping up in all the different subjects.

I also think that sexual tension had been built up through looking at some film advertisements which I saw in town. "Brutish" is what I always think when I see such pictures, but nevertheless, I stop and look at them.

All of these outside pressures and inside feelings resulted in tension which I tried to release in m. For me, m. always derives from sadness, never from happiness. But so far, I have just touched the surface of the problem.

On a deeper level it had to do with Arndt. I had told him, as you advised me, to turn to you with his "personal problems" as I termed them. But he didn't do it directly. He sent the letter for you in an open envelope to me and asked me to forward it. I read it. I shouldn't have done that. I understand now what you meant when you wrote that I, as a girl at my age, cannot help a fellow with this problem. I am now enclosing Arndt's letter which I couldn't get off my mind. And in thinking about it, m. tightened its grip on me.

But on the deepest level my bout with m. had something to do with my relationship to God. For quite a long time I have not read my Bible regularly and therefore my communication with God has been superficial. I have not been seeking his will for me, and I haven't been expecting him to speak to me through the Word of the Bible. God has seemed so distant and my prayers so empty.

The practical and visible expression of this inner situation was that I stopped practicing renouncing—not only sweets but other things as well. I simply have to admit that in behaving like this, I gave m. the opportunity to overpower me.

This is the first time I have really understood Genesis 4:7. The Revised Standard Version renders this rather dark verse, "If you do well, will you not be accepted? And if you do not do well, sin is crouching at the door; its desire is for you, but you must master it."

I would paraphrase it this way: "If you do well, Ilona, that is, if you are in contact with God, aren't you accepted then by God and doesn't that mean that you are able to accept yourself, and therefore master yourself and your desires? But if you do not do well, that is, if you are not in contact with God, then you open the door for sin. It is always crouching at the door, but only then you are vulnerable and feel its desire. Only then the tiger jumps and you can't master him any longer."

I just read the verse again and discovered that in the previous verse God asks Cain, "Why are you angry?"

Yes: Why was I angry?

That is the basic question. Not *that* I was angry at myself and the whole world around me. Rather *why* I was angry points toward my sin. My only answer is that I was out of touch with God.

There is no longer any doubt about it: M. is for me primarily an expression of a lack of communication with God, and therefore sin. Maybe it's different for other people. Then they will have to deal with it differently. But as far as my own life is concerned, m. is sin.

If I question this, it is the beginning of the end of my resistance. It is exactly as in the story of the Fall in Genesis 3 when the serpent tempted Eve by saying, "Did God say . . .?"

Before it happens, I say that m. is not sin for me. Afterwards I realize: If m. were not sin for me, I would do it every time I felt like it and I would become totally dependent on it.

Without the knowledge that it is sin, when I let m. happen I am in danger and unable to put a stop to it. I can only resist when this question is settled once and for all. I keep praying for another word that makes it crystal clear that it is sin for me.

I can also conclude this from the fact that I had to do it not only once but twice and even a third time. No, there doesn't exist for me—or in any case, not any longer—the case that it is "necessary." If it were really nothing more than a necessary release from tension, then why couldn't I stop after one time? Why would I have to repeat it?

It is exactly the same when it comes to sweets. When I have vowed not to eat any sweets for a day and then I do in spite of my decision, I eat a great deal. I guess I become defiant and feel that since I've already broken my promise,

I might as well really "live it up."

The same thing happens with m. I tell myself that I'll never be able to be a victorious Christian. I convince myself that I've already lost the battle, so I might as well give up. When I analyze my thoughts and feelings objectively, I realize that I create my own vulnerability.

Conclusion: When I open the door, I am overcome at once. No, I do not believe that I am capable of walking a tightrope. I would fall down immediately, as I just did.

This morning I read in Bonhoeffer's book *Living Together* the chapter on confession. I think that it would be really good for me to have such a cleansing talk with both of you just because it is harder for me to talk than to write. Therefore I would like to make the formal request for such a talk. Would it be possible to come and see you? I pray that I may be completely honest and not hold back anything out of shame.

So far you have never offered me such a talk, even though I sort of expected it. Your last letter helped me understand why: You did not want to give me the false expectation that confession would be like a magic wand solving all problems at once.

This letter contains my deepest thoughts, and it is in fact already a confession. All I have written I brought in prayer to my Lord last night. I simply cling to his word: "He who comes to me I will not cast out."

Father, thank you that I can come to you with all my guilt, not because my feelings tell me so, but because I know from your Word that you are faithful. Even when I am not faithful, you are. Thank you that you allow me to cast the burden of m. upon you and that I don't need to carry it with me all the coming days. Thank you that your grace is greater than my heart, and therefore I can ask you, "Lord, forgive me!" Thank you that you gave me the strength to write this letter.

July 24

Dear Ilona,

That was a great and profound letter! It showed us again that in the last count we are the ones who are being blessed through our correspondence with you.

We are relieved that you do not believe yourself capable of walking a tightrope. However, we are also happy that we did not forbid you outright to try. God himself has spoken to you, and that's why you must obey him and not us.

A thorough, cleansing talk is certainly a good place to begin. The time is ripe for you to take this step and we are very happy that we shall at last meet you face to face. We certainly cannot say that we have to "get acquainted" with you because we know you through your letters much better than we know many a person whom we meet every day.

We are especially glad that you want to come, even though you feel that such a talk is harder on you than writing to us. It is just for this reason that a personal confession is more helpful for many people than confessing alone to God or making a general confession in the church. However, it's not right to make a law about this and say that one can only experience forgiveness when confessing to God in the presence of a brother or sister in Christ.

A confessional talk is not necessary for salvation, but it often gives assurance of salvation. You see, the important thing is not the confession of sins but the pronouncement of forgiveness.

Arndt's letter is an indication of the confidence he feels in you. Otherwise he would have sealed his letter before enclosing it. But this openness on his part doesn't help you, as you say yourself. Neither could you help him if you were to write him about your own sexual problems. We do understand, though, what he wanted to tell you. The following phrases are meant especially for you.

"Up till now no one has ever noticed my inner life. How much I would wish for this in order to be freed from m."

This is a cry for help, directed to you. We understand too, now, why from the beginning he didn't want to build your relationship upon the physical level. He is hoping that you will help him turn away from the physical to what he calls the "inner life." Somehow a boy needs a girl in order to make this change of direction.

That's why you wouldn't help him if you were to encourage a physical relationship with him out of pity or as a means of "therapy." We do not have the impression, though, that this is your intention. But we wanted at least to mention it, because some people think that intercourse is a remedy for m. On the contrary, we believe that it would hinder Arndt from becoming a man who has learned to handle his sexuality—to say nothing of other problems which would come up and bring you both in a still greater conflict with your conscience.

The questions which you asked us at one time about the

sexual difficulties of a young man have now been answered by a very concrete example. You can see, as with yourself, that the lack of contact with one's parents plays an important role. Arndt's contact with his father is not even mentioned. The contact with his mother is mentioned only in a negative sense because she, as a doctor, was more occupied with her profession than with her children. We were deeply moved by his sentence: "She left me as I was. Certainly I loved her, but I could not show her my love."

Since Arndt did not ask any questions, no one spoke with him. That's why his first nocturnal emissions (wet dreams) gave him a shock—just as the first menstruation would to a girl who was not expecting it. His classmate in boarding school, who introduced him to masturbation, had an easy job, especially since Arndt never received praise from his teachers and therefore sought refuge in this comfort substitute.

His letter, by the way, can also clarify for you why it is harder for a young man to master his sexuality than it is for a girl. At a certain stage in his development, m. is less avoidable for him than for a girl. Girls often have no idea what they do to young men when they turn them on sexually.

You can also see from his letter how unsure a boy is of himself and how much more boys are afraid of girls than the other way around. During a certain period in his life Arndt felt so base and sinful that he didn't even dare approach a girl. It was a big step for him when he opened up to you.

In conclusion we would like to quote these lines from Arndt's letter, because they sound like a preparation for our talk: "When I was sitting in church after confession, I felt God very close to me, even within me. This feeling never came back again. . . . How much I would like to know again his touch and experience the magnificent consciousness of being a virgin!"

When will you come?

Dear Mr. and Mrs. T.,

Actually I had intended to call you last night to tell you how thankful I am for everything you have given me. But it is too difficult to express this on the phone, and that is why I am writing you. Thank you for taking time for me and for all the love you have given me.

The verse stands on my desk: "He that has clean hands grows stronger and stronger" (Job 17:9). It has become "my" verse; it shall guide me from now on, and I will always remember it when it seems that God is far away from me.

I had often wondered what it was like to repent. Now I know. It is something wonderful. To have such a conversation with God in front of witnesses can have a powerful effect on one's everyday life. It is power, in every sense of the word. God's forgiveness has been given to me—if I may put it this way—not as something self-evident that automatically follows sin but as a help which encourages one on the way. I received the deep assurance that Jesus also died for me. Everything which still needed to be straightened out with my parents and brothers and sisters has been done, and I have also asked them for forgiveness.

I am especially thankful for the fact that I was able to get to know you, Ingrid. Simply through your being, through the peace and joy that you radiate, I caught a glimpse of what it means to accept one's self, without reserve, as a woman. Now I am more sure than ever that self-acceptance is the decisive key in solving the problem of m.

I am beginning to understand what it means "to let the tiger into the living room." When I am involved in doing something now, I often remind myself that I am involved as a *woman*, with all the strength and beauty that my sex carries with it. I finally realize the difference between genital activity on the one hand and self-acceptance and involvement as a sexual being on the other.

The essay by Mary Stewart which you enclosed was a great help to me. I reread it again on the train. I was especially struck by the sentence, "I wanted God's Spirit more than I wanted physical titillation." I had to ask myself, "Ilona, which do you desire more?"

I also found helpful the author's discussion of her sexual daydreams and how she learned to entrust them to God. I can directly relate to this because when sexual desire becomes very strong (which generally occurs the week before I have my menstruation), I daydream a lot. I also want to give these fantasies to God so that I will be able to say, "I desired all things that I might enjoy life. God gave me life that I might enjoy all things."

However, I find it difficult to identify with Mary Stewart on one point. She experienced a clear turning point in her life. She said, "*Before* I got to know Christ I felt fear, loneliness, etc. . . . *Afterwards* it was totally different—and as I did not want to lose this, I changed my behavior."

But I never experienced such a turning point. Actually, I can't ever remember life *without* God. For me there have only been progressing stages, marked by milestones— such as my cleansing talk with you. But it seems to be a very gradual growth process for me, one with lots of valleys. Sometimes I am reminded of a wheel; one spot is always touching the earth (hitting a low point) before it continues on its way up and around. The only other option is, of course, for the wheel to remain motionless.

I know, however, that it is ridiculous to compare my walk with God with someone else's. God deals with each of us in a unique and personal way. I remember what you said during our conversation: "God doesn't build prefabricated houses that all look the same. There are no carbon copies in God's kingdom."

When I returned home, I found a letter awaiting me from Arndt. He is pressing me for a more decisive commitment. He says it is impossible for him to wait four years without having more assurance about the outcome of our relationship. He desires more than just a friendship and wants to come and talk things over.

I do not think that this is a good idea. It is premature— like picking a fruit before it is ripe. I need time to grow and find myself before I can make any binding decisions. I also want to finish my studies, and I will just have to explain all of this to him.

I am going to ask him not to consider me as his "girl friend" but rather as a friend. I think it is possible to have companions and friends of the opposite sex, just as we do of the same sex. Sure, this is also "walking a tightrope," but I think I can handle this one. In the meantime, you know that I have turned nineteen and I think that it's about time to grow up.

Of course, my heart still longs for a deeper relationship that gives comfort and security. But just a few days ago I found a card with the following text. The words of encouragement will help me to endure the tension and longing I feel. I will also send this verse to Arndt: "Only the things you can wait for are really important."

Postlude—a dialogue with the reader

Frankly, we would be happy if all of your questions were answered by now. We would like to think that you have found enough practical hints in this correspondence so that you can find your own way. However, if you find that a very personal question has been left unanswered, you may also write to us.

We are sure that you would still like to know one thing: How did Ilona fare after the last letter published here?

During the following two years our exchange of letters became less frequent. She became more independent and wrote that she would not need m. any more. It was too superficial for her, practically meaningless. She said that she had learned to enjoy deeper feelings and to say yes to her womanhood: "I am happy that I am still free and see so many possibilities to learn and to grow." Discipline in her schedule, she said, was one of her greatest helps. Twice she slipped again as she called it, but that did not hinder her "to keep on living undismayed and cheerful."

When we called her to ask whether she would agree to publishing our correspondence some day—a thought which naturally had never entered her mind—she asked for a day to think it over. Then she wrote,

"If God is so great that he can even use my guilt and failures to help others, I can only—gratefully and trustfully —say yes. The thought that these letters should be my property alone has burdened me already. This is why I am glad that I don't have to keep them for myself and can share them with others. At the same time the publication will be a challenge to me to stick to that which I have experienced as a help and to live that which I recognize as being true."

We ask you to join us in thanking Ilona by interceding for her.

Walter and Ingrid Trobisch
A-4880 St. Georgen,
Austria, Europe

Appendix I

THE TIGER STORY
(from *I Loved a Girl*)

Dear Francois,

It is almost midnight. But I want to answer your letter right away.

You write that Christ hasn't heard your prayer. I ask you, what did you pray for? That he would deliver you from being a man? What do you want? To be without sex? To have no more desire at all?

What you speak of is not possible. All that one does, one does either as a man or woman. Your sexuality is in your waking and sleeping. It is present with you when you work and when you pray. In your holiest feelings and in your purest prayers it is there.

If you believe in Christ, then you know that your body has become the temple of the Holy Spirit. If you pray for the mutilation of the temple, then Christ will not hear you. Christ wants to make you capable of living with your manhood.[22]

Must the one who believes flee from love? I know there are many Christians who withdraw themselves and who turn their backs on it. They avoid the opposite sex and think by doing so that they are especially mature and redeemed Christians.

They fool themselves. He who believes does not flee.

You can't run away from your manhood: it belongs to

you; it is a part of yourself.

Let me tell you a story:

Once upon a time there was a tiger. He was captured and put in a cage. The keeper's task was to feed him and guard him.

But the keeper wanted to make the tiger his friend. He always spoke to him in a friendly voice whenever he came to his cage. The tiger, however, always looked at him with hostility in his green, glowing eyes. He followed every movement of the keeper, ready to spring on him.

The keeper was afraid of the tiger and asked God to tame him.

One evening, when the keeper had already gone to bed, a little girl got lost in the vicinity of the tiger's cage and came too near to the iron bars. The tiger reached out with his claws. There was a blow, a scream. When the keeper arrived he found dismembered human flesh and blood.

Then the keeper knew that God had not tamed the tiger. His fear grew. He drove the tiger into a dark hole where no one could come close to him. Now the tiger roared day and night. The terrible sound disturbed the keeper so that he could no longer sleep. It reminded him of his guilt. Always in his dreams he saw the torn body of the little girl. Then he cried out in his misery. He prayed to God that the tiger might die.

God answered him, but the answer was different from what the keeper had expected. God said, "let the tiger into your house, into the rooms where you live, even into your most beautiful room."

The keeper had no fear of death. He would rather die than go on hearing the roar of the tiger. So he obeyed. He opened the door of the cage and prayed: "Thy will be done."

The tiger came out and stood still. They looked into each other's eyes for a long time. As soon as the tiger noticed that the keeper had no fear and that he breathed quietly, he lay down at his feet.

That is the way it began. But at night the tiger would begin to roar again, and the keeper would be afraid. So he had to let the tiger come into his house and face him. Again he had to look the tiger directly in the eye. Again and again. Every morning.

He never had the tiger completely in his power "once and for all." Again and again he had to overcome him. Every day brought the same test of courage.

After some years the two became good friends. The keeper could touch the tiger, even put his hand between his jaws. But he never dared to take his eyes off the tiger. When they looked at each other they recognized each other and were glad that they belonged together and that each was necessary to the other.

Francois, you have to learn to live with the tiger, courageously, eye to eye. For that purpose Christ will set you free.[23]

SEXUAL FREEDOM
V. Mary Stewart

If at the time I came to Christ I had known and acknowledged as God-given all of the various constraints on sexual activity, I probably would not have gone a step further in my walk with him. If I had known the extent to which he would "put his spirit within me and *cause me to walk in his statutes*" (Ezek. 36:27), patiently, gently breaking down the accumulated habits of twenty-seven years and gradually replacing them with exactly the constraints (or, as I now see them, *freedoms*) I have just listed —well, I would have thought twice about going on this Christianity trip.

Because, you see, I was a very liberated young woman at the time. I had had a rich sexual fantasy life almost since I could remember. I had learned to masturbate efficiently at a very young age. I had almost lost count of the number of men I had slept with in a serially monogamous fashion. I had taken advantage of the spirit of the Women's Movement (in which I was quite active) to begin exploring my own bisexuality. And I had no intention of giving any of that up. When I accepted Christ, I figured that it was the spirit of the law, not the letter, that mattered, that "love" was the overriding principle, and that I could witness in bed as easily as anywhere else.

But to my progressive astonishment, I found all that changing. Not quickly. Not all at once. Not by anyone's prying into my personal life or trying to send me on a guilt-trip (although I am sure I had lots of people praying for me). It was totally a process of God's working on me, one item of behavior at a time, over many months, like patiently peeling one layer after another off an onion.

He accomplished this in two ways. First of all, much like some of David Wilkerson's ex-addicts who really *tried* to return to drugs and found they could not get high anymore, I found that I was getting progressively less satisfaction from my sexual behavior. The various pleasures simply started to be less and less worth the effort and hassle associated with them. Second, I began to sense a correlation between my own behavior and thoughts, on the one hand, and the closeness and reliability of God's peaceful presence, on the other. Gradually, the nature of the correlation became clear: To the extent that I indulged in my "liberated" sexual behavior any given day or week, to that extent did I find myself, in all other areas of my life, thrown right back into the feelings of anxiety, rush, fear and turmoil that had been so dominant a part of my life before coming to Christ. To the extent that I *did not* indulge (even if it was only because I was too busy doing other things), to that extent did I find God's energizing and peaceful presence available to me.

In a nutshell, God's spirit and presence had become the ultimate positive reinforcer for me, and the more I had of it, the more I wanted. If maintaining that presence meant that other (now less satisfying) reinforcers had to go, then I was willing to let them go. I am not saying that there was not at times struggle or ambivalence, or that the process had not included a lot of prayer and a lot of stumbling. My over-riding feelings, however, are *not* ones of being "deprived" or "punished," but rather of being progressively liberated, gentled and strengthened. One of Peter's epistles tells us that "a man is the slave of whatever has mastered him" (2 Pet. 2:19). In other words, to the extent that the caprices of my sexuality dictated my thoughts, motivations and actions in my pre-Christian life (which was all too often the case) rather than my controlling my own behaviors, I was a slave.

Sleeping Around

Not surprisingly, the first layer of the onion that the Lord set to work on was my sexual behavior with other people. I began to see (and again, without any other person prompting me) that the need to be always in a sexual rela-tionship with someone really did not have that much to do with the release of sexual tension. Rather, it was a des-perate fight against a rarely admitted loneliness and isola-tion; it was the best (or only) way I knew how to approxi-mate some reassurance that somehow, for a little while anyway, there was a semblance of commitment, caring and communication. Very simply, it was an attempt to fill that "God-shaped void" of which Pascal wrote. Over the weeks and months that I still tried to get the best of both worlds, that is, tried to be a Christian and still sleep around, I reached two conclusions. The first was that while I had never had any trouble *attaining* that desired commitment and communication, I was never able to *maintain* it. It was always the same way: A fellow and I would start out with a tremendous euphoric closeness which sooner or later became empty and ritualized. We would go along playing the game for a while, but finally one or the other of us would pull out, determined that next time it would be different. It never was.

The second thing I learned was that feeling isolated has little to do with whether or not one is sharing a bed with someone, or even trying to share a life. I cannot count the nights I have lain awake, sometimes muffling sobs in a pillow, beside a satiated, soundly sleeping male, wondering why I was feeling so alone. It was not that the men in question were doing all the taking and not giving—I did not specialize in relationships like that. Mostly they were people who themselves wanted a real and pretty total relationship. But somehow, just because we were trying to get it all from each other, we ended up having even less than we started with, feeling only constraint instead of communication. Somehow we were running the relationship on the wrong fuel.

On the other hand, I will never forget the tremendous liberation I felt the first night I had enough strength in the Lord to say No and not feel any need to apologize for it or rationalize it. I remember how good it felt to fall asleep *alone*, in my own bed, by myself, and how overjoyed I was to wake up in the morning and confirm that no one was there beside me. I have never felt *less* isolated in my life—then, or ever since.

Masturbation

As if it was not surprise enough to find myself quite happily foregoing sexual contact with other people, I found the Lord starting to convict me about having it with myself! Now, the Bible does not have anything very explicit to say about masturbation, and there seem to be lots of Christians who endorse it as good safety-valve behavior and as a way of getting in touch with your own sexuality. But aside from the fact that the fantasies which almost inevitably accompany masturbation clearly constitute lust and hence (if we take the Sermon on the Mount seriously) are tantamount in God's sight to the act itself, there are quite sound psychological reasons why masturbation is neither "good practice for the real thing" nor even a good safety-valve. I will try to explain them.

Sexual arousal has tremendous conditioning potential; it can attach itself to whatever stimulus it has been associated with in the past, and if continually paired with that stimulus, it will ultimately *require* that restricted stimulus pattern in order to be evoked at all. This is the way that the more peculiar sexual anomalies get built up. For example, a boy whose first stirrings of sexual arousal came in the context of seeing women's underwear may thereafter call up the image of women's underwear whenever he wants to re-evoke the original sexual "rush," and in order to aid masturbation. Ultimately, after years of such restricted associating, he finds he cannot get turned on *unless* he has women's underwear around. Hardly a liberating state of affairs.

I began to realize that a similar, if somewhat less exotic, process accompanies masturbation. Most people enhance and catalyze this behavior with specific, favorite fan-

115

tasies whose content gradually comes to be closely associated with orgasm. As a result, the goal in sexual contact with another person becomes approximating the content of these fantasies as closely as possible. Now, no earthly reality can compete with a fantasy. Reality just is not that conveniently flexible. Sometimes it may be better, sometimes worse, but for sure it will almost never be the *same* as the fantasy. The best you can do is *use* the other person as the means of approximating the "perfect" experience that you conjure up in your head when you are alone, and as a result the act becomes little more than mutual masturbation—no contact other than the physical, and probably poor even in terms of mere bodily, let alone psychological, gratification.

So, surprising as it may seem, and contrary to the canons of most of our present-day sexologists, I would maintain that the more sexually "naive" you are coming to the marriage bed, the more *eventual*, reliably mutual psychic *and* physical satisfaction there will be. These are some of the thoughts that came out of that period of weeks and months when the Lord reoriented my thinking and behavior about masturbation, and the ultimate result was the same as it had been regarding the issue of sleeping with others: I eventually stopped—again, not without struggle and stumbling, but I stopped. I wanted God's Spirit more than I wanted transient physical titillation, and, over and above that, I began to see that abstinence made sense in terms of optimal preparation for *real* sharing with a *real* person.

Fantasies

Finally, as if I was not surprised enough to have happily abandoned both fornication and masturbation, God began to prompt me to relinquish my casual thoughts and fantasies even when they were not linked to specific behaviors. At first this seemed like too much. Sexual fantasies are one of those things that almost everyone indulges in constantly. (One study found that students of both sexes, by self-report, spent up to a quarter of their work time sexually fantasizing). Fantasies are a way of coping with boredom, fatigue, frustration and anxiety, and as such seem very functional. So why not fantasize?

Why not indeed, if the events and contingencies of our real world are merely random happenings, "full of sound and fury signifying nothing," as Macbeth put it. If God does *not* "work all things together for good to those who love him and are called according to his purpose" (Rom. 8:28), and if he *does* let chance bring us its share of purposeless boredom, irritation and pain, then it would seem that the most healthy and functional reaction would be to withdraw temporarily into a world of pleasant fantasizing, sexual or otherwise.

But on the other hand, if he is as good as his Word, if he is the God of history (both the history of the world and of each of his reborn children in it), if he desires to work *all* the realities (pleasant and unpleasant) of a Christian's life together in a meaningful way with the end result that we are conformed to his image and copartners in his purposes for eternity, then to me it seems that grappling with *whatever* reality confronts me will in the end be infinitely more exciting than a retreat into any kind of fantasy. I myself am finding this to be gloriously so. (That is a nice thing I have discovered about God: If you test out his promises even hypothetically and conditionally, he lets you know he means business.) In fact, I do not want to miss out on *any* good things he has in store for me, even if it sometimes means doing spiritual calisthenics when it would be easier to grab onto an immediate, pleasant fantasy in order to evade or postpone some boring task or anxiety-provoking commitment.

Again, my batting average is not perfect. My trust in the Lord is still shaky at best, and there are times when I still prefer to believe that my solutions are better than his. Invariably, though, he proves me wrong, and I am learning fast. That is why I have abandoned even my fantasies, and that is why I do not even miss them.

The Joy of Life

The amazing thing about this whole process of progressively giving over to God all my sexual behavior and thoughts is that I have ended precisely where Scripture says I should be: a single woman, sexually quiescent, but not feeling the least bit unsexed—even though I myself would never have voluntarily submitted to the house-cleaning process in the first place had I know what it would involve. The Lord is a gentle schoolmaster. His yoke is easy and his burden is light. He never came down hard on me or required me to work on more than one area at a time. He never withdrew his Spirit capriciously or arbitrarily, but was always there, merely waiting for *me* to move closer back to *him* after each stumbling and seeming al-

118

ways to rejoice at my return. He provided the most wonderful Christian brothers and sisters to share my struggles and to pray me through to each new plateau—always with love and never with condemnation.

Furthermore, I found that he never shortchanges anybody: For each "toy" he asked me to give back to him, he had something better in return, the fruit of the Holy Spirit: love, joy, peace, patience, kindness, gentleness, purpose and a progressive integration of all aspects of my life. To some, particularly those who are single or those who feel that they can never be fully heterosexual, these may seem like inadequate substitutes for those great sexual "rushes" that come from calling up mental fantasies and seeking out physical contact; but to those readers, I would simply say: Don't knock it till you've tried it, and given it a fair chance in terms of time and consistent effort.

Jesus came to give us life and to give it more abundantly (Jn. 10:10). He has never said that sexuality was bad; he only asks that we trust him with that function of our lives no less than with our material welfare, our vocation, our social interactions or our family relationships—all of which are equally and awesomely significant reinforcers that we would all, in the flesh, dearly love to control by ourselves. Until we can open our tightly clenched fists, he cannot fill our hands full to overflowing. Unless we can trust his rewards to be better than anything we could possibly provide for ourselves, we will be settling for second-best nourishment and wondering why we still feel deprived. "I desired all things, that I might enjoy life; God gave me life, that I might enjoy all things."[24]

119

NOTES

Notes

[1] See Schulte/Tölle, *Psychiatrie*, 2nd ed. (New York: Springer-Verlag, 1973), p. 125.

[2] Horst Wrage, *Mann und Frau* (Gütersloh: Gerd Mohn Verlag, 1916), p. 69.

[3] Ibid., p. 159.

[4] Ibid., p. 86.

[5] See Cornelius Trimbos, *Leben mit der Liebe* (Germany: Matthias Grünwald Verlag).

[6] See Seymour Fisher, *The Female Orgasm* (New York: Basic Books, 1972), p. 336.

[7] Ibid., pp. 235 and 278.

[8] See Affemann, *Geschlechtlichkeit und Geschlechtserziehung in der modern Welt* (Gutersloh: Gerd Mohn Verlag, 1970), pp. 87ff.

[9] See Appendix I.

[10] Affemann, p. 139.

[11] Walter R. Johnson, *Masturbation, Siecus Study Guide No. 3,* (New York: Sex Information and Education Council of the United States, 1968), p. 7.

[12] Ibid., pp. 73 and 88.

[13] Ingrid Trobisch, *The Joy of Being a Woman* (New York: Harper and Row, Jubilee Books, 1975).

[14] Fischer, pp. 334ff.

[15] See H. J. Prill, *Psychosomatische Gynäkologie* (Germany: Verlag Urban and Schwarzenberg), p. 35.

[16] See Walter Trobisch, *Love Yourself: Self-Acceptance and Depression* (Downers Grove, Ill.: InterVarsity Press, 1976).

[17] See *The Joy of Being a Woman.*

[18] Ernst Lange, *Die Zehn grossen Freiheiten* (Gelnhausen: Burckhardt-haus Verlag, 1965), p. 7. The translation is Ilona's. This book is also available in English as *Ten Great Freedoms,* trans. David Priestley (Downers Grove, Ill.: InterVarsity Press, 1970).

[19] See Helmut Thielicke, "Anthropologische Grundtatbestände in individuellen Konfliktsituationen," *Zeitschrift für Evang. Ethik* (May 1974), p. 140.

[20] Gini Andrews, *Your Half of the Apple* (Grand Rapids: Zondervan, 1972), pp. 94-95.

[21] See Appendix II which reprints a portion of this article.

[22] See Dr. Hans Burki, *Glaubenswelt und Liebenslieben* (Zurich: Vereinigte Bibel Gruppen).

[23] Reprinted from *I Loved a Girl* (New York: Harper and Row, 1965), pp. 74-76.

[24] Reprinted from V. Mary Stewart, *Sexual Freedom* (Downers Grove, Ill.: InterVarsity Press, 1974), pp. 9-20.